Presented To

_____

"The Lord bless you and keep you; the Lord make His face shine on you." Numbers 6:24-25 NKJV

From

_____

Copyright ©2024 by Barbara Austell a.k.a. B Waites Austell and Steve Austell.
Revised Edition 2025.
Cover design created by B Waites Austell using elements from Canva, glitter background by F.A. from Starlight via Canva, cover image HC 112024-01-from Harper, an AI developed by OpenAI.
Activity art created by Steve and B Austell.

Printed in the United States of America| 10 9 8 7 6 5 4 3
ISBN (paperback): 978-1-7347930-8-6
ISBN (hardback): 978-1-7347930-9-3
ISBN (ebook): 979-8-9920959-0-6

Simply B You® is a registered trademark and may not be used without permission.

All rights reserved. No part of this book, either in electronic form or paperback, may be reproduced or transmitted in any form or by any means mechanical or electronic, including photocopying, recording, or by any information storage and retrieval system without written permission from the publisher.

Special Acknowledgment: Collaborative assistance provided by Harper, an AI developed by OpenAI, for cover image and interactive activity formatting enhancements.

Scripture Acknowledgments:
Scriptures taken from the **New King James Version**®. Copyright©1982 by Thomas Nelson. Used by permission. All rights reserved. Scripture taken from the **HOLY BIBLE, NEW INTERNATIONAL VERSION**®. Copyright®1973, 1978, 1984 International Bible Society. Used by permission of Zondervan. All rights reserved. Holy Bible, **New Living Translation**, copyright © 1996, 2004, 2015 by Tyndale House Foundation. Used by permission of Tyndale House Publishers, Inc., Carol Stream, Illinois 60188. All rights reserved. Unless otherwise indicated, all Scripture quotations are taken from **The Living Bible**, copyright © 1971 by Tyndale House Foundation. Used by permission of Tyndale House Publishers, Carol Stream, Illinois 60188. All rights reserved. Scriptures taken from the **Holy Bible, New International Reader's Version**®, NIrV® Copyright © 1995, 1996, 1998, 2014 by Biblica, Inc.™ Used by permission of Zondervan. Scripture quotations marked AMP are taken from the **Amplified® Bible (AMP)**, Copyright © 2015 by The Lockman Foundation. Used by permission. All rights reserved. www.lockman.org. Accessed via Bible Gateway at www.biblegateway.com. Scripture quotations marked GW are taken from GOD'S WORD® Translation (GW).
 Scripture quotations taken from the Easy-to-Read Version © 2006 by Bible League International. Used by permission. All rights reserved. Accessed via www.BibleGateway.com.

Simply B You, LLC | Simply B
Franklin, TN 37067
www.SimplyBYou.com

Dedication

Dedicated to our daughter, son-in-law,
and precious grandchildren.

To Lisa, the wise and faithful friend, Chris, the biblical life application Pastor, Jill, our wonderfully creative friend, Dr. Sandy and Reverend Shane, and Dwight—the Ultimate Life Coach.

And to all those who seek to draw closer to God, may this devotional inspire and strengthen your journey of faith.

Devotional Days

Day 1: Strength in Weakness
Day 2: Trusting God
Day 3: God Knows Your Name
Day 4: Blessings upon Blessings
Day 5: Humbleness
Day 6: Faith in My Life
Day 7: Me and My Thoughts
Day 8: Speaking Life
Day 9: Living by Faith
Day 10: Renewed Energy
Day 11: Every Step is for Him
Day 12: God Knows Our Needs
Day 13: Don't Worry
Day 14: Goodness Follows Me
Day 15: Pray more
Day 16: Gardens
Day 17: Following God
Day 18: Where's My Treasure
Day 19: Give
Day 20: Study and Meditate
Day 21: God's Rain
Day 22: Debt
Day 23: Simply Family
Day 24: God Builds Our House
Day 25: Doing the Right Thing
Day 26: Think Before You Speak
Day 27: Words Have Power
Day 28: Mouth Filters
Day 29: Just Love Me
Day 30: Thoughts
Day 31: Accomplished by God
Day 32: What About Love?
Day 33: Finding a Safe Place

Personal Note

Dear Reader,

From Dr. B:
Thank you for embarking on this 33-day journey with us. This devotional grew from my personal journey where I experienced the three key tests of faith: health, wealth, and family. I was dealing with a severe illness. You know, I was hoping that I'd be well at the end of the 33 days. I experienced something even more profound. I experienced that my attitude toward what I was going through at the time changed! You see, my mind needed a shift. It needed to be shifted to where I was more focused on the things of God than other things. It was in my heart and mind that I needed to journal specifically for 33 days.

The number 33 carries profound significance—it's a number of healing, ministry, and transformation. Jesus was 33 when He began His ministry, and He bore 33 stripes on His back so that we could walk in healing. These 33 days are designed to help you reflect on God's promises, grow in faith, and experience personal breakthroughs.

From Steve:
This devotional isn't just a book—it's an invitation to live intentionally with God at the center. Each day challenges us to reflect, realign, and move forward in our faith. As you read, I encourage you to take it one step at a time, knowing that God is working in ways you can't yet see. Remember, He's a God of completion.
We're praying for you! This 33 days of devotional time are about more than reading the words on the page. It's your time to embrace transformational change.

With love and prayers,
B & Steve

Founder of Simply B You®
www.SimplyBYou.com

Introduction

This devotional is designed to guide you through three key tests of faith—Health, Wealth, and Family. Each section invites you to trust God in areas that often challenge us the most. These scriptures have been a great source of comfort and guidance for us. We hope you'll also make them a part of your life.

Part 1: Health is about trusting God with all of us: mind, body, and soul. Health challenges can be stressful for you, your family, and your finances.

Part 2: Wealth focuses on financial stewardship, challenging us to align our resources with God's purposes. Money can be a source of stress or a tool for blessing. This section invites you to see wealth through God's eyes. Financial stress can also be challenging for your health and your family.

Part 3: Family explores the joys and challenges of family life, emphasizing the importance of making God the foundation of our homes. Strong families endure the seasons of life challenges.

Throughout the book, interactive Christian coaching activities offer practical steps to apply to your life. We hope you'll walk away from this journey with a renewed trust in God. We pray that your perspective will be shaped by God as you draw closer to Him.

Part 1: Journey of Faith for Health

In this journey of faith, health is the first key test that challenges us to trust God with every part of our lives—body, mind, and spirit. True health goes beyond physical well-being; it involves emotional, mental, and spiritual wholeness. In the same way that God cares for every detail of our spiritual lives, He also cares deeply about our physical and emotional health. Our bodies are temples of the Holy Spirit, and we are called to steward them well, knowing that God desires us "to prosper and be in good health, just as our souls prosper" (3 John Verse 2 NKJV).

There will be moments when our health wavers, when sickness, stress, or unexpected challenges threaten our well-being. It's in those times that our faith is tested. We are invited to believe in God's promises of healing and to rely on His strength, even when we can't see the results right away. As you engage with these devotions, remember that God is the ultimate Healer, who renews our energy, restores our strength, and empowers us to live the full, abundant life He has promised.

Part

Health

Day

1

"God wants us to give Him our broken pieces and that's where the healing begins."
Dr. B

Strength in weakness

"No weapon formed against you shall prosper. .."
Isaiah 54:17 NKJV

Life is full of challenges, but take heart—God is always with you. Isaiah 54:17 says no weapon formed against you will prosper. This doesn't mean you won't face hard times, but it does mean those challenges won't defeat you. "God is your protector, and His strength is made perfect in your weakness" (Psalm 46:1 and 2 Corinthians 12:9 NKJV).

God's power steps in when we feel weak. Trust Him. He sees what you're going through and already has a plan for your victory. Stand firm in His promises, knowing that nothing can overpower the God who loves and defends you.

Confession
I confess that I am healed by the blood of the Lamb. No weapon formed against me will stand.
Complete healing is mine.

Prayer
Lord, I thank You for Your protection over my life. I stand firm in Your promises when challenges come my way. Surround me with Your peace and strength, and help me trust that You are fighting every battle for me.
In Jesus' name, Amen.

Reflection Moments: God's Promises

On the outside of the shield: List challenges that you've faced over the past month or so.

Inside the shield: Write God's promises of protection and victory.

God's Promises

Coaching Exercise: Victory Steps

Do you need a breakthrough? Please take a moment to write down the areas in your life that are troubling you the most.

_____
_____
_____
_____
_____
_____

Take a moment to pray. Now, write your personal prayer for breakthrough that you need in your life.

_____
_____
_____
_____
_____
_____

Day

2

"Your health. Your life. Continue to excel in both."
Steve

Trusting God

"Then your light will break forth like the morning your healing shall spring forth speedily. And your righteousness shall go before you; the glory of the Lord shall be your rear guard."

Isaiah 58:8 NKJV

God's healing power is real in this world. Isaiah 58:8 tells us that healing will come like the morning light, bringing hope and strength. His righteousness goes ahead of you, making way for your breakthrough. His glory is behind you. Protecting you. His healing is not just physical; it is also healing of our mind and spirit.

Confession
I confess a speedy and complete healing.

Call to Action
Lord, I call forth your healing power over life.

Reflection Moments: Trust Ladder

Step 1: Write five breakthrough steps on the ladder below. On each step, write a small action or mindset shift that will help you trust God more.
example: Start my day with prayer.

Step 2: Reflect on past victories.
At the top of the ladder, write a goal that represents fully trusting God in a specific areas of your life.

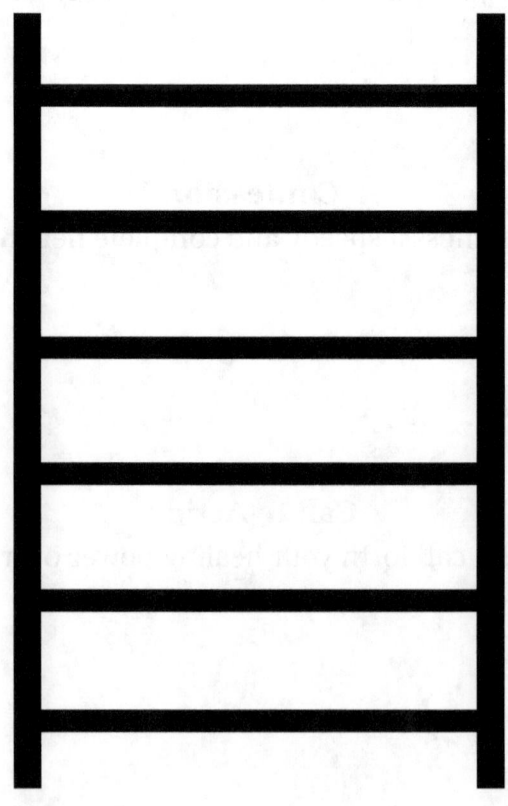

Coaching Exercise: Trusting God

List three areas in your life where you are seeking God's healing (physical, emotional, or spiritual). Next to each, write one practical step you can take to trust God more in that area.

_____
_____
_____
_____
_____

Write a prayer for strength or even a letter to God.

_____
_____
_____
_____
_____

Day

"Sometimes we need to listen to hear God call us by name!"
Dr. B

God knows your name

"Now when He had said these things, He cried with a loud voice, "Lazarus, come forth!"

John 11:43 NKJV

Just like Jesus called Lazarus by name, He knows your name, situation, and heart. When He called, Lazarus had no choice but to respond, even from death. The same God who spoke life into Lazarus is speaking life into you today. You may feel bound by circumstances, illness, or fear, but know this: God's power is greater than anything trying to hold you back. His voice breaks every chain. As you trust Him, speak healing over yourself and believe His power is at work, calling you to rise up and walk in wholeness. Throw off the grave clothes binding you when He calls your name.

Confession
I confess with my mouth, my heart, my soul, my mind, spirit and every fiber of my being that I'm healed.

Prayer
Lord, I call forth your healing power over life.

Reflection Moments: Affirmation Map

Write your name in the center, surrounding it with affirmations from God's Word. What are your favorite verses?

_____

_____

Coaching Exercise: Embrace Your Identity

What does God calling your name mean for your purpose?

_____
_____
_____
_____
_____
_____

It's your turn! Write your own personal affirmation over your life.

_____
_____
_____
_____
_____

Day

4

"Live the promise!"
Dr. B

Blessings upon blessings

"Beloved, I pray that in every way you may succeed and prosper and be in good health [physically], just as [I know] your soul prospers [spiritually]."

3 John Verse 2 AMP

We have great news to share with you today. God's promises cover every aspect of our lives—spiritually, physically, and emotionally. He desires not only for us to prosper in our souls but also to experience His goodness in every area. Living the promise means walking in faith, knowing God's Word is true, and aligning our lives with that truth. Receiving God's promises can be hard for us sometimes. It's all about having a mind-set shift to accept the promise and then live it out in our daily lives.

Confession
I confess that we live the example of the promise.

Prayer
Lord, we call forth the promises that You have for our lives. Help us to live the example.
In Jesus' name. Amen.

Reflection Moments: Promise Tracker

In the first column: List promises from Scripture that speak to your heart about the health of you or a family member.

In the second column: Write how you've experienced or hope to experience these promises.

God's Promises **My Life**

Coaching Exercise: Aligning with the Promise

What's one area of your life where you feel disconnected from God's promises?

Write a simple action step to align your thoughts or actions with His Word.

_____
_____
_____
_____
_____
_____

Finish with this affirmation:
I choose to live the example of God's promise today. Feel free to use the space provided below to write your own personal affirmation/positive statement over your life.

_____
_____
_____
_____
_____

Day

"Humble yourself to hear God's voice."
Steve

Humbleness

"Then if my people which are called by my name, will humble themselves and pray and seek my face and turn from their wicked ways, then I will hear from Heaven, and will forgive their sin and heal their land."

II Chronicles 7:14 NKJV

God promises to bless when we humble ourselves before Him. Humility is key to hearing from God. When we set aside our pride and trust Him fully, He guides us, blesses us, and meets our needs. Wealth is more than just money—it's having peace, joy, and health in all areas of life. As we humble ourselves, pray, and seek God, He opens the doors of His blessings.

Confession

Father, we are committed to doing the three things that you ask. We humble ourselves and we know we need to pray. We have turned to you. Forgive us for the time in our life where we did not seek your face before we made our plans for our life. We honor and worship you as You are the Lord of our lives.

Prayer

Lord, show us how to be humble.
In Jesus' name. Amen.

Reflection Moments: Heart Check

Divide the heart shape shown below into two sections by drawing a line down the center.

On one side: Write areas where you feel self-reliant.
On the other side: Write ways you can rely more on God.

Coaching Exercise: Humility in action

Think of one area in your life where you can invite God's guidance. What is it? Write your commitment in the spaces provided below and share it with us and your friends. Let's inspire each other!

_____
_____
_____
_____

Commit to one act of service this week. What will it be?
Will you encourage someone either that you know or don't know? Will you offer to help at a community event, such as a food drive or a clean-up campaign? Will you pray for someone either over the telephone or perhaps via text, offering them comfort and support?

_____
_____
_____
_____

Day

"Don't be afraid to hope!"
Dr. B

Faith in my life

"...God who gives life to the dead and calls those things which do not exist as though they did."

Romans 4:17 NKJV

Faith isn't just believing in what you can see. It's trusting God for what's unseen. There were several times in my life when I was so sick that I was almost afraid to hope! I couldn't see or feel my healing, but knew to continue believing. Romans 4:17 reminds us that God brings life to what was once dead and calls what doesn't exist into existence. Hope is the foundation of faith, and even when situations seem impossible, we can trust that God is at work.

Don't be afraid to hope! God's promises are alive and powerful! Speak life over those dead things in your life, believing that God is already bringing healing and restoration. Let your faith rise up inside you. Trust in the God who makes the impossible possible. My attitude toward what I was going through changed before I saw the change in my life.

Confession
I confess that I not only hope but I believe that God is healing all of the dead things in my life.

Prayer
Lord, please bring Your Promises into my life.
In Jesus' name. Amen.

Reflection Moments: Testimonial Time!

Think of a past experience where God worked in an unexpected way. Write a short "faith story" to remind yourself of His power to bring life and hope.

Please write down 3-4 names of the people you wish to share this story with this week. You never know who God will place in your path where that person needs to be encouraged by your special story.

1.
2.
3.
4.

Coaching Exercise: Faith Vision Board

Think about where you want to be in 33 days from now. Take time to write down how you envision your life. What do you plan to change?

_____
_____
_____
_____
_____

What about this time next year? Feel free to write down the pictures or items you wish to collect to create an actual board.

_____
_____
_____
_____
_____

Day

"Keep your thoughts on God
and
your faith will grow."
Steve

Me and my thoughts

"...For as he thinks in his heart, so is [he in behavior...]"
Proverbs 23:7 AMP

What we think builds and shapes how we live. Those things will appear if we fill our minds with worry and doubt. But if we focus on God's promises, our faith will grow, and we will see His blessings unfold. When it comes to wealth, it's not just about money. It's about living with a mindset of abundance, knowing that God will provide. Keep your thoughts centered on Him. Trust that He will meet your needs and grow your faith.

Confession
I confess that my behavior aligns with your Word.

Prayer
Lord, please help me ensure that my thoughts are
on You.
In Jesus' name. Amen.

Reflection Moments: Thought Inventory

Take a few moments to reflect overs some of the thoughts that you've had over the past week or so.

Please write them in the space provided.

Negative	Positive

Coaching Exercise: Mind-Set Shift

Choose one negative thought from your list. Rewrite it as a positive, faith-filled thought.

_____
_____
_____
_____
_____

Commit to meditating on this new thought throughout the day. Write down the way you choose to *actively* meditate on this new thought.

Will you think about it while you're on a walk? Maybe working out? Cooking dinner?

_____
_____
_____
_____
_____

Day

"Speak God's Word. See new life!"
Dr. B

Speaking life

"Then he said to me, "Speak to these bones for me. Tell them, Dry bones, listen to the word of the Lord!"
Ezekiel 37:4 ERV

God's Word has the power to bring new life to dead places. In Ezekiel 37:4 God told Ezekiel to speak to the dry bones. We are called to speak life into the areas that seem lost or hopeless. It's not about what we see in the natural. It's about trusting that things will change when we declare God's Word over our situation. This trust in God's healing power brings a sense of reassurance and security, knowing that He is always at work.

There was a time when I faced uncertainty about ever walking again after surgery on my left leg. For 24 weeks, I had to persistently "speak" to my leg, declaring healing even when I couldn't see it. Like in Ezekiel 37:4, where Ezekiel spoke life to the dry bones, I had to speak life to what felt dead. God healed my leg, but the healing didn't come immediately. It was a powerful reminder that God's Word brings life, even when we can't see it immediately. So, I encourage you to speak boldly to the dry bones in your life and trust that God is at work.

Confession
I confess with my mouth that the dead bones in my life are being brought back to life.

Prayer
Lord, please help me speak to the dead and dry bones in my life and trust You.
In Jesus' name. Amen.

Reflection Moments: Life-Giving Word Map

Let's create a word map.
1) Write specific areas in your life that need renewal.
2) Next to each area, write a corresponding Bible verse or promise.

Daily Practice: Choose one area and spend 1-2 minutes declaring the verse aloud, visualizing God's restoration.

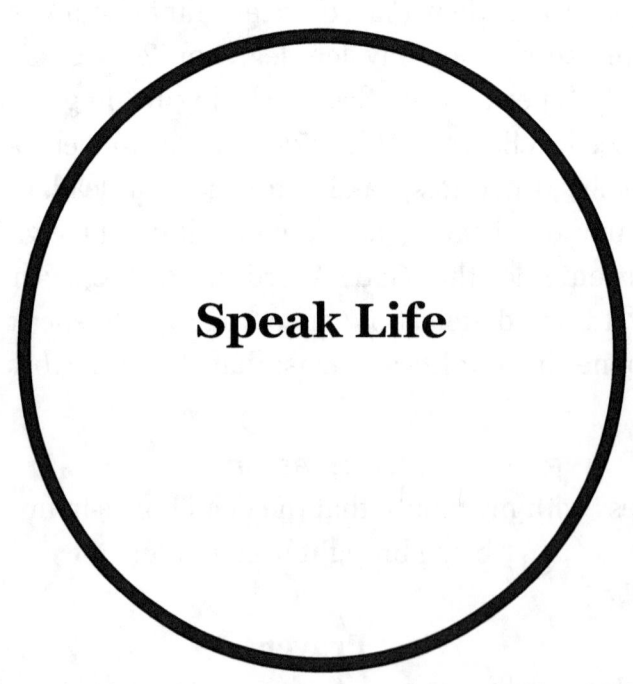

Coaching Exercise: Speak Life Challenge- Voice Activation

Record and Replay:
Record yourself on your phone or another device declaring a positive statement over one area of your life that needs renewal. Write it in the space provided. Replay it daily to remind yourself of God's promises.

_____

_____

_____

_____

_____

Powerful Pair-ups: Find an accountability partner (friend or family) to exchange declarations. Encourage each other to speak life and celebrate small victories.

Fun Twist: Set a daily "Speak Life" alarm with your declaration as the alarm name. When it goes off, speak your declaration boldly! Write your plan in the space provided below.

_____

_____

_____

_____

_____

Day

9

"Standing in faith for a change in my life."
Steve

Living by faith

"But He was wounded for our transgressions, He was bruised for our iniquities; The chastisement for our peace was upon Him, And by His stripes we are healed."

Isaiah 53:5 NKJV

Jesus was wounded and bruised for our sins. By His stripes we are healed. Jesus is not just a distant figure. He is our personal healer. He desires to be involved in every area of our lives, including finances and health. He took on our pain and struggles so we could receive peace, joy, and abundance. Stand in faith for the change you need in your life. Thank Jesus for what He's done and receive all the good things He has for your life.

Confession
I confess that I'm healed whether I feel it or not.

Prayer
Jesus, thank you for what You did for me! I receive ALL of the good things for my life.
In Jesus' name. Amen.

Reflection Moments: Faith Walk Timeline

Draw a timeline of key moments in your life where you've seen God's faithfulness. Leave space for future "faith milestones."

Coaching Exercise: Faith in Action

What's one area where you need to step out in faith?

_____
_____
_____
_____
_____

Write a specific action you'll take this week as a step of faith. Reflect on how trusting God impacts your outlook.

_____
_____
_____
_____
_____

Day

10

"Energy is a gift from God."
Dr. B

Renewed energy

"Yet, the strength of those who wait with hope in the Lord will be renewed. They will soar on wings like eagles.
They will run and won't become weary. They will walk and won't grow tired."

Isaiah 40:31 GW

Imagine someone just handed you a beautifully wrapped gift. Inside the box was energy. It was divinely given and perfectly timed. God doesn't intend for us to live life worn out and drained. As an Energy Management Coach, I've really seen God work in people's lives to renew their energy! He promises us the strength we need to live fully for Him. Energy is a precious gift from God, a resource that we should be grateful for, regardless of mental clarity, physical strength, or spiritual status. Take this moment in time set aside to recognize and actively utilize the energy He's given you. Speak it over your life, and thank Him for this gift that sustains you in every season.

Confession
I confess that I have this promised energy to live my life the way that God intended!

Prayer
Lord, thank you for this gift of energy!
In Jesus' name. Amen.

Reflection Moments: Energy Audit

Divide the page into "Drains" and "Renewals."

Drains: List activities or thoughts that deplete your energy.

Renewals: List things that recharge you spiritually, mentally, or physically.

Drains   Renewals

Coaching Exercise: Energy Alignment

Choose one "drain" to minimize today.
Replace it with a "renewal" activity.

What will you choose to work on? Please write in the space provided.

_____
_____
_____
_____
_____
_____

Reflect: How does this shift improve your energy and focus on God?

_____
_____
_____
_____
_____
_____

Day

11

"You don't need a vehicle to travel the Word of God."
Steve

Every Step is for Him

"Jesus went all over Galilee. He taught in the synagogues and spread the Good News of the kingdom. He also cured every disease and sickness among the people."

Matthew 4:23 GW

God's Word is a powerful force that brings transformation and healing wherever it goes. We can carry His promises to others, bringing hope and faith. We don't need fancy or eloquent phrases; His Word is enough. We find healing, hope, and the strength to face today's challenges when we embrace God through His Word.

Trust that His Word is enough. I believe in His healing power and I've experienced it in action in my life. His Word is an anchor in the stormy seas of life. Trust in God will help you to navigate the sometimes stormy seas of life.

Confession
I confess that no matter how I feel that I know that You heal.

Prayer
Lord, thank you for this gift of healing. Help me accept today's challenges.
In Jesus' name. Amen.

Reflection Moments: Word Walk

List ways God's Word has guided your life. Leave space to add more over time.

Coaching Exercise: Step by Step

What's one step you can take today to share God's Word with someone else?

Write it down and commit to taking that step.

_____
_____
_____
_____
_____

Write a prayer for the person that you've chosen.

_____
_____
_____
_____
_____

Part 2: Key Test of Faith-Wealth

Wealth is the second key test of faith that we want to discuss. This is a pain point for many because it challenges us to trust God's provision in our finances. The Bible often speaks about wealth. It can be a powerful tool to honor God and bless others. True wealth isn't just about money; it's about aligning our financial life with God's purposes. God's Word teaches us to be faithful stewards of our resources. Just remember, everything we have/own comes from Him.

Life doesn't always go according to plan. There may be seasons of financial struggle due to job loss, unexpected health expenses, or other challenges. Yet, even in those moments, God invites us to trust Him, lean on His promises, and create a plan. Financial wisdom isn't about being stingy or selfish. It's about making choices that reflect God's heart and using what He's given us to make a difference.

In this section, you'll be reassured that God's guidance is always available for your financial decisions. Managing your finances by cultivating a mindset of contentment and using wealth to bless others has the potential to enrich your personal spiritual journey. There are more ways to view wealth than just a number in your bank account. Think about the treasure you're storing in heaven when you bless others.

Part 2

Wealth

Day

12

"Ask God."
Dr. B

God knows our needs

"And my God will meet all your needs according to the riches of His glory in Christ Jesus."

Philippians 4:19 NIV

God knows our needs before we even ask. Philippians 4:19 reminds us that He provides not out of scarcity but according to His abundant riches in glory. We may face moments when our circumstances seem overwhelming, but faith calls us to trust that God is already at work. Ask God. He is faithful to provide for every need, big and small. We see promises in action when we lean on His provision and align ourselves with His truth. Today, no matter what you're facing, trust that God will meet your needs in ways beyond what you can imagine.

Confession
I believe that God will supply all my needs, no matter what my circumstances look like in this moment.

Prayer
Lord, I trust You to meet every need I have today. Help me to lean on Your provision and not be swayed by my circumstances. I thank You for Your faithfulness and the abundance You provide.
In Jesus' name. Amen.

Reflection Moments: Needs vs. Blessings Bingo

Let's have some fun today. We know that talking about finances can be stressful. It doesn't have to be that way! Reflect on how God meets your needs and surprises you with blessings. Mark a square as you take a moment to think of ways that God has met your needs and ways that you still need His help.

Draw some pictures to indicate needs vs blessings.

♡ Heart shape=Need/s   🎁 Gift Box=blessings

Needs vs Blessings

♡				
				🎁

Coaching Exercise: Gratitude Walk

Take a short walk (indoors or outdoors) and reflect on God's provision.

During the walk, pause to thank God for each need He has met in your life.

_____
_____
_____
_____
_____
_____

Jot down some of your thoughts that you had during your walk.

_____
_____
_____
_____
_____
_____

Day

13

"Seek God. Not the need."
Steve

Don't worry

³¹"Don't worry and say, 'What will we eat?' or 'What will we drink?' or 'What will we wear?' ³² That's what those people who don't know God are always thinking about. Don't worry, because your Father in heaven knows that you need all these things. ³³ What you should want most is God's kingdom and doing what he wants you to do. Then he will give you all these other things you need."

Matthew 6:31-33 ERV

God knows what you need. Seek Him. Watch Him care for the rest. He reminds us not to worry about what we eat, drink, or wear. We're called to focus on Him. He promises to provide everything when we put God's kingdom first. It's easy to get caught up in life's needs and forget to seek God.

Confession
I trust You, Lord, with everything in my life.

Prayer
Lord, help me trust You even when I feel anxious about my life. In Jesus' name. Amen.

Reflection Moments: Mind Map

Label the center of the circle as "God's Peace."

Around it: Write down your worries as smaller circles, connecting them to the center with lines.

As you **pray**, draw an "X" over each worry, symbolizing surrendering it to God.

Coaching Exercise: What's My Verse?

Identify a verse to recite whenever you begin to worry.

Take a moment to write the verse in the space provided.

_____
_____
_____
_____
_____

Write a different version of the verse. For example, use the Message version for the verse that you selected.

_____
_____
_____
_____
_____

Day

14

"Trust God."
Dr. B

Goodness follows me

"Surely goodness and mercy shall follow me all the days of my life: and I will dwell in the house of the Lord for ever."

Psalm 23:6 KJV

God's mercy and His love are not distant promises, but immediate realities for today. Psalm 23:6 reassures us that His goodness is always with us. It's not about striving to earn His blessings. It's about trusting and dwelling in God's presence. This means we have faith that God will provide for our needs. Trusting God means we can rest in His perfect peace and provision. Today, know that you are constantly wrapped in His love.

Confession
I have goodness and mercy following me. I live and dwell in the presence of God.

Prayer
Lord, You know my needs even before I do. I trust in Your perfect provision.

In Jesus' name. Amen.

Reflection Moments: Goodness Hunt

Take a "Goodness Walk" (indoors or outdoors). As you walk, note down anything that reminds you of God's goodness and mercy, a kind interaction, nature's beauty.

Write down these observations on the page as a reminder of His daily presence.

Observations:
1.
2.
3.
4.

Coaching Exercise: Blessings Ripple Effect

Create a Ripple Map:
Make a list in order of a ripple effect that starts with family, friends and even strangers.

_____
_____
_____
_____
_____

Challenge:
Track the ripple effect—encourage recipients to "pass it on" and reflect on how small blessings spread widely

_____
_____
_____
_____
_____

Day

15

"Pray more. Worry less.
God has you."
Steve

Pray more

⁶"Don't worry about anything; instead, pray about everything. Tell God what you need, and thank him for all he has done. ⁷ Then you will experience God's peace, which exceeds anything we can understand. His peace will guard your hearts and minds as you live in Christ Jesus."

Philippians 4:6-7 NLT

Life can feel overwhelming. We open the door to God's peace and presence when we share our needs and thank Him for what He's done. This peace goes beyond what we can understand and will guard our hearts and minds. God wants us to trust Him with our worries. He cares about every detail of our lives. So today, choose to pray more and worry less, knowing that God has you in His hands.

Confession
I release my worries to God because He cares for me!

Prayer
Lord, I bring all my concerns and needs before You with a thankful heart. I trust in Your faithfulness and Your plan for my life. Let Your peace fill my heart and mind where there's no room for worry.
In Jesus' name. Amen.

Reflection Moments: Prayer Chain

In each loop, write a prayer request or concern. As prayers are answered, shade in or decorate the corresponding loop to visually track God's faithfulness.

Coaching Exercise: Gratitude Ladder

Write something you're grateful for: starting from small daily blessings at the bottom rung of the ladder and moving up to the larger life blessings at the top.

Write a short reflection about how climbing this "ladder" helps shift your mindset from worry to peace.

_____
_____
_____
_____
_____

Day

16

"Lord, send Your rain."
Dr. B

Gardens

"The Lord will guide you continually, And satisfy your soul in drought, And strengthen your bones; You shall be like a watered garden, And like a spring of water, whose waters do not fail."

Isaiah 58:11 NKJV

There are seasons when life feels dry, but God's promise is to refresh and guide us, no matter what. Isaiah 58:11 reminds us that God is present, even in the driest places, ready to strengthen and sustain us. Like a well-watered garden, we flourish not because of perfect circumstances but because of His constant provision. When we ask, "Lord, send Your rain," we invite Him to renew our weary souls.

I was invited to a retreat in a state known for its "desert-like" conditions. A drought had persisted for quite some time. I carried my umbrella with me because I trusted God to rain on me physically and spiritually. He did! He provides what we need by turning dry ground into fertile soil. Trust in His timing and faithfulness.

Confession

I declare that God is guiding me and providing for me in every season. Even in dry places, He strengthens me and refreshes my soul.

Prayer

Lord, thank You for being my constant guide and provider. I trust You to meet all my needs even when I walk through difficult times. Strengthen me and refresh my spirit, so I may flourish like a well-watered garden.
In Jesus' name. Amen.

Reflection Moments: Well Watered Garden

Draw or describe a garden that represents your life when nurtured by God's Word.

Coaching Exercise: Nurture Your Garden

What's one area in your life that needs "watering"?

_____
_____
_____
_____
_____
_____

Write an action step to prioritize spiritual growth in that area.

_____
_____
_____
_____
_____
_____

Day

17

"Follow Jesus."
Steve

Following God

"The Lord is my shepherd; I have all that I need."

Psalm 23:1 NLT

God blesses us when we act with intentional generosity. It's the giving promise found in Luke 6:38, "returned to us in abundance, pressed down, shaken together, and running over." But this isn't just about money; it's about giving grace, love, and forgiveness. We are rich in His blessings, grace, and forgiveness when we freely give. I recall hearing a Pastor once say, "You can't outgive God." Trust God to fill your life with His good gifts as you honor Him by giving your talents, time, and money.

Confession
I confess with my mouth, my heart, and my mind that
The Lord is my Shepherd.

Prayer
Lord, You are my shepherd. I trust in Your care. I thank You for meeting my needs and guiding me with Your wisdom. Help me to rest in Your provision.
In Jesus' name. Amen.

Reflection Moments: Shepherd's Path

The simple path as shown below illustrates Jesus leading as your Shepherd. Mark key points where you've experienced His guidance.

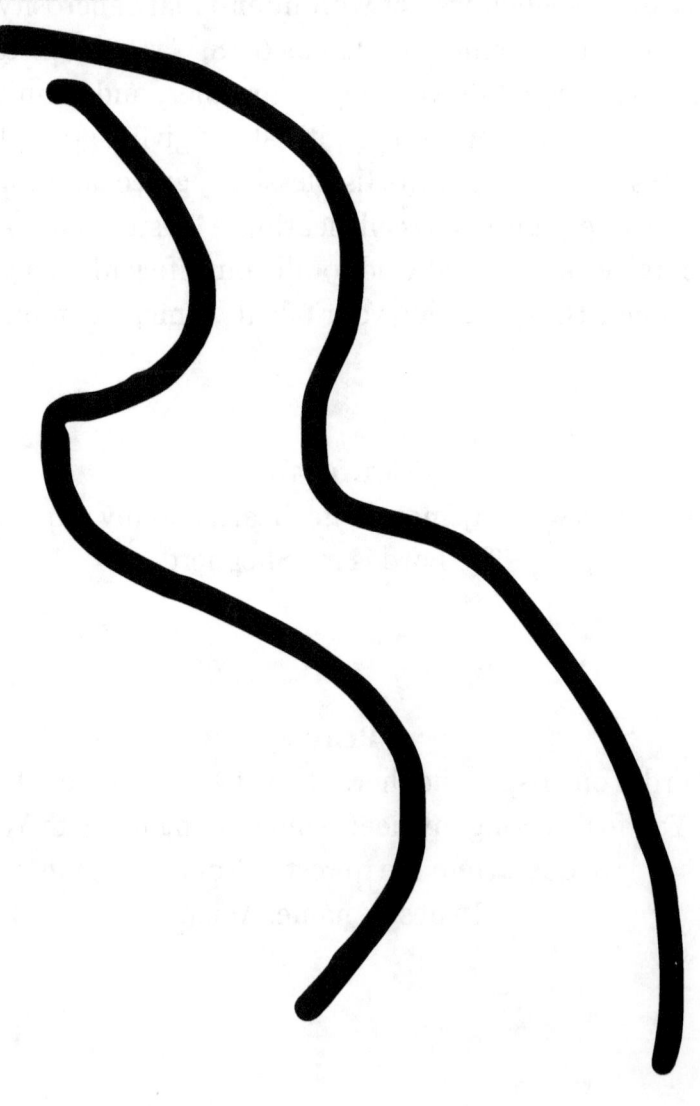

Coaching Exercise: Following Steps

What's one decision you need to trust Jesus with this week?

_____
_____
_____
_____
_____

Write it down and commit to praying about it daily.

_____
_____
_____
_____
_____

Day

18

"What's in your heavenly treasure box?"
Dr. B

Where's my treasure?

[19] "Don't store up treasures here on earth, where moths eat them and rust destroys them, and where thieves break in and steal. [20] Store your treasures in heaven, where moths and rust cannot destroy, and thieves do not break in and steal. [21] Wherever your treasure is, there the desires of your heart will also be."

Matthew 6:19-21 NLT

Coming from a low socio-economic background, I struggled with this concept at a time in my life. I didn't place material possessions before God, but they were important to me. It's not that God doesn't want us to have nice things—He does! He blesses us abundantly, beyond what we can imagine. But it's about using those blessings with wisdom.

We store up treasures that can never be stolen or destroyed when we invest our time, energy, and focus on God's kingdom. Ask yourself, "What's in my heavenly treasure box?" Let go of distractions like excessive materialism, unhealthy relationships, or negative habits that don't last. Embrace what matters most. Your heart will follow where you place your treasure. Let it lead to God's promises and His purpose!

Confession
I choose to focus my thoughts on God's promises.

Prayer
Lord, help me to value the things that matter most—Your kingdom and Your purposes. Teach me to let go of earthly distractions and to store up treasures that last forever.
In Jesus' name. Amen.

Reflection Moments: Treasure Box

Fill the box with what you consider your heavenly treasures. (faith, family, acts of kindness)

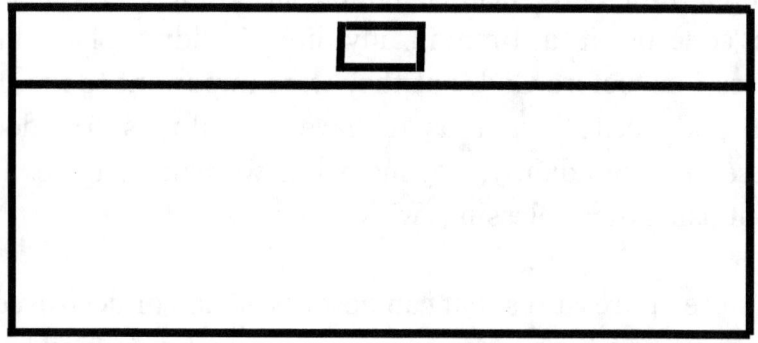

Coaching Exercise: Shifting Focus

Identify one earthly distraction you'll minimize this week.

_____
_____
_____
_____
_____

Write how focusing on heavenly treasures impacts your mindset on a daily basis.

_____
_____
_____
_____
_____

Day

19

"God's abundance is never ending."
Steve

Give

"Give, and it will be given to you: good measure, pressed down, shaken together, and running over will be put into your bosom. For with the same measure that you use, it will be measured back to you."

Luke 6:38 NKJV

God's blessings overflow in our lives when we give with a generous heart. We've already talked about this concept, giving is an important part of our humanity. It's about giving grace, love, and forgiveness. We are rich in His blessings, grace, and forgiveness when we freely give. Trust Him to fill your life with His goodness as you give to others.

Confession
I am rich in His blessings, grace, and forgiveness.

Prayer
Lord, help me learn how to be a better giver.
In Jesus' name. Amen.

Reflection Moments: Overflow Journal

List blessings you've received and ways you can pass them on to others.

1.
2.
3.
4.

Coaching Exercise: Giving Plan

Reflect on how giving blesses you and others.

_____
_____
_____
_____
_____

Reflect on how giving blesses you and others.

_____
_____
_____
_____
_____

Day

20

"Success starts with staying in God's Word."
Dr. B

Study and meditate

"Study this Book of Instruction continually. Meditate on it day and night so you will be sure to obey everything written in it. Only then will you prosper and succeed in all you do."

Joshua 1:8 NLT

Aligning our lives with God's Word should be our only measurement of success. Joshua 1:8 reminds us that we'll find true success when we meditate on Scripture day and night. The transformative power of God's Word is not to be underestimated. Reading the Bible gives us guidance, and strength for every challenge. It's not about rushing through a reading plan but letting God's truth sink deeply into our hearts. I like to think about it like this: don't treat your Bible Study time like you're in a drive-through line. We may indeed have more time than others on some days. My advice is to pray and ask God to bless your time together.

Our faith and understanding grow when we dedicate our minds to the study and meditation of Scripture. Won't you join us today in a commitment to meditating on a verse or a section of scripture today?

Confession
I will study and meditate on the Word of God.

Prayer
Lord, help me set my mind to study and meditate on Your Word.
In Jesus' name. Amen.

Reflection Moments: Scripture Focus

Choose a verse and meditate on it. Write down what God reveals to you.

What did you learn?

Coaching Exercise: Daily Study Habit

Set a daily time to study God's Word. Tip: Add an alarm to your phone or schedule it as a meeting on your calendar.

_____
_____
_____
_____
_____
_____

Write how this habit can bring spiritual success.

_____
_____
_____
_____
_____
_____

Day

21

"God's abundance is never ending."
Steve

God's rain

"The Lord will send rain at the proper time from his rich treasury in the heavens and will bless all the work you do. You will lend to many nations, but you will never need to borrow from them."

Deuteronomy 28:12 NLT

God's abundance is plentiful. He blesses our human efforts in ways that we can't begin to imagine. His supply is infinite, and His promise of more than enough, is unwavering. This provides us with a sense of security and confidence. It also gives us hope for a stronger financial future.

Confession
I confess that I believe that You have my financial future in Your hands.

Prayer
Lord, please help me to practice wisdom in the area of finances.
In Jesus' name. Amen.

Reflection Moments: Rain of Blessings

Draw some more raindrops and write blessings you're praying for within each drop.

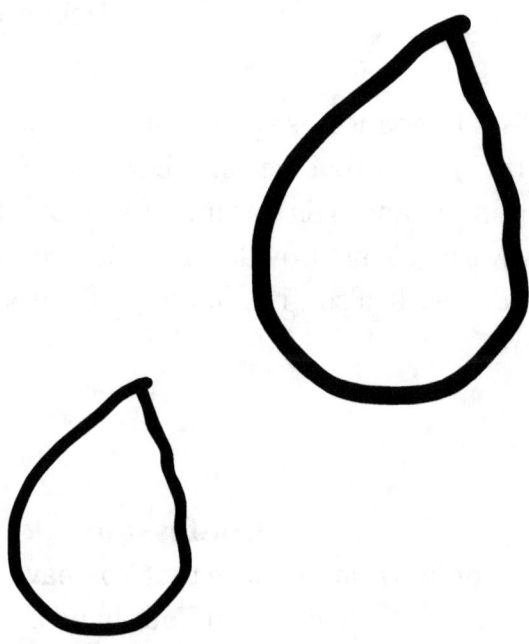

Coaching Exercise: Blessing Exercise

From your left-hand page, select one of the blessings you're praying for. Create Your Growth Plan: Write an action step you can take to align with God's provision for this blessing. Examples: 1) If praying for financial provision: I will create a budget and stick to it. 2) If praying for family harmony: I will schedule weekly family prayer time."

_____
_____
_____
_____
_____

End with a written prayer or declaration acknowledging God's abundant provision: Feel free to write your own or add to this one.

Lord, I trust that You will send the rain of blessings at the perfect time.

_____
_____
_____
_____
_____

Day

22

"Financial management isn't selfish. It's practicing wisdom for what God has given you."
Dr. B

Debt

"Owe nothing to anyone—except for your obligation to love one another. If you love your neighbor, you will fulfill the requirements of God's law."

Romans 13:8 NLT

Financial management can be a sensitive topic. Sometimes, we find ourselves in debt due to circumstances beyond our control, such as a job loss or health challenges. It's not about blame. Financial management isn't selfish.

It's about honoring God with what He's given you through the practical application of wisdom. We may also gain wisdom through reading and praying. We can also gain knowledge by accepting financial coaching and learning to enhance our financial management skills. Romans 13:8 reminds us to "owe nothing except love."

Confession
I'll do my best to stay with the financial plan that You've helped me to create so that I can be debt free.

Prayer
Lord, please align my life with Your will.
In Jesus' name. Amen.

Reflection Moments: Debt Freedom Tree

Roots: Label them with the "causes" or reasons for your current debts (financial, emotional, or spiritual).

Trunk: Write your foundational goal ("Freedom through Christ").

Branches: List the "fruits" or benefits of freedom (peace, stability, generosity).

Coaching Exercise: Freedom Accountability Partner

Identify a Partner: Write down someone you trust to hold you accountable on your journey to freedom.

Set Milestones: Create 2-3 small, achievable milestones with deadlines. Example: Pay off $100 of debt this month.

_____
_____
_____
_____
_____

Let's celebrate! Plan a small reward for achieving each milestone and reflect on how each step deepens your faith.

_____
_____
_____
_____
_____

Part 3: Key Test of Faith-Family

Family is the third key test of faith that we will explore during our time together in this devotional. God created the family unit as a reflection of His love for us. Now, sometimes our family life can be filled with joy, growth, and sometimes even challenges that keep us on our knees in prayer. The beauty of it is that each family has its unique story. These stories may become our testimonies. Psalm 127:1 reminds us that our efforts are in vain unless the Lord builds our house.

In this section, you'll find encouragement to rely on God's promises for your family, to pray fervently, and to allow Him to be the foundation that holds everything together. Family life is an ongoing faith journey from navigating difficult conversations to celebrating milestones.

Let's build a home where God's love, patience, and forgiveness reign. As you go through these devotions, remember that God's hands are on your family as He guides and protects through every season.

Part 3

Family

Day

23

"Don't be afraid to be the spiritual leader of the household."
Steve

Simply family

"...But as for me and my family, we will serve the Lord."
Joshua 24:15 NLT

Don't be afraid to step into the role of the spiritual leader of your family. It doesn't mean having all the answers. It's simply setting the example by seeking God, praying, and putting Him first in your life.

Your family looks to you for guidance. You build a strong foundation for their faith when you show them what it means to serve the Lord. Trust God to help you lead with wisdom, love, and courage.

Confession
Lord, help us keep our family centered on You.

Prayer
Lord, please hold us close in Your loving arms.
In Jesus' name. Amen.

Reflection Moments: Family Tree of Faith

Let's work on your family tree of faith. Start with yourself at the center. Add branches for parents, grandparents, children, and other family members as applicable.

Mark God's Presence:

Next to each family member, note significant moments where God's presence, blessings, or guidance were evident

(example: Mom's healing in 1998, Family prayer tradition started by Dad). Use symbols or colors to represent different types of blessings (hearts for love, crosses for spiritual breakthroughs, stars for answered prayers).

Reflect: Look at your tree and write a short prayer of gratitude for how God has worked in your family's story.

Coaching Exercise: Family Spiritual Leadership Plan

Identify Your Leadership Style: Write down your top strengths as a spiritual leader (teaching, encouraging, hospitality). **Reflect** on how these strengths can benefit your family.

Choose one specific action to take this week (lead a family devotion or prayer). Schedule a family community project.

_____
_____
_____
_____
_____
_____

Create a Spiritual Leadership Contract: Write a short, empowering contract to commit to your goal.

Include: Your goal and how you plan to hold yourself accountable. Feel free to reach out to a close friend or mentor to ask for help.

_____
_____
_____
_____
_____

Day

24

"Do you know your house builder?"
Dr. B

God builds our house

"Unless the Lord builds a house, the work of the builders is wasted."

Psalm 127:1 NLT

Building a strong family starts with a solid foundation. There's no better foundation than God. Psalm 127:1 reminds us that all our efforts are in vain if the Lord isn't the builder of our home. It's easy to rely on our own strength, but true strength comes from trusting God to hold us together.

No matter what we face, He is the builder who keeps our family connected. Today, remember that God is the cornerstone of our house—our source of stability, love, and guidance. Lean into His strength and trust Him to build a home that lasts.

Confession
Lord, You are the foundation of our house.

Prayer
Lord, please help us to remember that in You we find our strength to be held together as a family.
In Jesus' name. Amen.

Reflection Moments: God Builds Our House

Write how God strengthens your family by using the sections below (foundation, walls, roof). Write how God strengthens your family. Feel free to draw your own house.

Coaching Exercise: Foundation Check

What's one area in your family life that needs God's strengthening?

_____
_____
_____
_____
_____

Write an action step to invite God into that area.

_____
_____
_____
_____
_____

Day

25

"Include God in your family activities."
Steve

Doing the right thing

"I have singled him out so that he will direct his sons and their families to keep the way of the Lord by doing what is right and just..."

Genesis 18:19 NLT

God singles out Abraham to lead his family in the ways of the Lord. We are called to do the same with our families. Including God in your family activities doesn't have to be complicated.

It can be as simple as praying together, reading a Bible verse, or discussing how God works in your lives. Inviting God into your daily routines strengthens your family's faith and creates lasting bonds.

Confession
I confess that I'll teach my family about You.

Prayer
Lord, please help us to do the right thing for You.
In Jesus' name. Amen.

Reflection Moments: Spiritual Leaders

- Each family member selects a role for the week.
- Rotate roles weekly to keep everyone engaged and invested.

List the names.
- Prayer Leader
- Scripture Reader
- Encourager
- Hospitality

Coaching Exercise: Simply Talk

Ask each family member to share a short story where they've seen God's presence in their life (an answered prayer or a situation where, perhaps a stranger, gave encouragement or positive words).

_____
_____
_____
_____
_____

Write down key points from each story to create a shared Family Faith Storybook.

_____
_____
_____
_____
_____

Day

26

"You can't rewind a conversation and delete the words that you've spoken."
Dr. B

Think before you speak

"...take note of this: Everyone should be quick to listen, slow to speak and slow to become angry,"
James 1:19 NIV

Words are powerful—they can build up or tear down, and they can't be taken back once spoken. James 1:19 reminds us to be quick to listen and slow to speak, urging us to pause before responding.

I've learned that you can't rewind a conversation and delete your spoken words. I really-really struggle in this area. A moment of reflection can save a lifetime of regret. Today, let's commit to being intentional with our words, speaking life instead of hurt. Trust God to guide your speech. Let your words reflect His love and wisdom in every conversation.

Confession
I confess that I'll think before I open my mouth to speak.

Prayer
Lord, please help us realize that our words are powerful.
In Jesus' name. Amen.

Reflection Moments: Thinking Before You Speak Words Inventory

Step 1: Try to think back over the past week or month about things that you've said. I know that can be challenging! Hang in there! I promise that it's worth it!

Step 2: For positive words, include phrases that encouraged or uplifted others.
For Harmful Words, list any words spoken in frustration, criticism, or negative tone in the Not so positive column.

Positive Words	Not Positive Words

Coaching Exercise: Pause and Reflect

Practice a 5-second pause before speaking today.

Write how pausing impacts your communication.
Track Your Words:

_____
_____
_____
_____
_____

What patterns do you notice?
How did your words impact the people around you?

_____
_____
_____
_____
_____

Day

27

"Be forever thankful with your thoughts and words."
Steve

Words have power

"The tongue has the power of life and death, and those who love it will eat its fruit."

Proverbs 18:21 NIV

Our words have incredible power. What we say can either build up or tear down. In our families, it's important to speak words of life, encouragement, and thankfulness.

Being thankful with both your thoughts and words creates a positive environment for your family to grow in love and faith. When we express gratitude and speak life over our loved ones, we invite God's blessings into our homes.

Confession
I confess that I understand the importance of paying attention to what I say.

Prayer
Lord, please help me pay attention to my thoughts and the words that I speak.
In Jesus' name. Amen.

Reflection Moments: Power Statements

Write 3 life-giving statements you can speak over your family or yourself daily.

1.
2.
3.

Coaching Exercise: Speak Life Challenge

Commit to speaking only positive, faith-filled words for 24 hours.

_____
_____
_____
_____
_____

Reflect on how it changes your environment.

_____
_____
_____
_____
_____

Day

28

"Lord, guard my words with Your wisdom because I know my mouth filter slips sometimes."
Dr. B

Mouth filters

"Set a guard, O Lord, over my mouth; Keep watch over the door of my lips."

Psalm 141:3 NKJV

Our words can be powerful, for better or worse. There are days when my "mouth filter" slips, and I'm reminded of the importance of seeking God's wisdom before I speak. Psalm 141:3 is a heartfelt prayer asking God to guard our lips. It's a humble acknowledgment that we don't always get it right, but we can rely on His guidance.

Today, let's commit to being intentional with our words, choosing love and wisdom even when it's hard. Ask God to help you speak words that uplift and encourage, reflecting His grace to everyone you meet.

Confession
I confess that I will be diligent with the words I use throughout the day.

Prayer
Lord, please help me find loving words to speak over those people that you put in my path.
In Jesus' name. Amen.

Reflection Moments: Mouth Filter Check

Create a checklist of phrases that align with God's Word and those that need filtering.

1.
2.
3.
4.

Coaching Exercise: Daily Filter Practice

Pray each morning: "Lord, guard my mouth today."

_____
_____
_____
_____
_____

At the end of the day, journal how God helped you filter your words throughout the day.

_____
_____
_____
_____
_____

Day

29

"Have compassion for everyone."
Steve

Just love me

"By this all will know that you are My disciples, if you have love for one another."

John 13:35 NKJV

Compassion is a key part of love within our families. I try really hard to think about how my words will impact other family members. It's easy to say something in anger and regret it later. Sometimes, we tend to be nicer to strangers than our own family members. Let's practice listening to the needs of everyone around us. Caring for the needs of those around us. Prioritize others and offer grace and kindness even when it's hard.

I had a situation recently where someone said some very hurtful things to me during a meeting. It discouraged my day and almost spilled over into my family life. However, I chose to show grace to that person. Extending grace from one's heart to another can be a powerful turning point in your life.

Confession
I will do my best to love everyone.

Prayer
Lord, please help me love everyone.
In Jesus' name. Amen.

Reflection Moments: Compassion Map

List family members or friends.
1.
2.
3.
4.

Next to each name, write a simple act of love or compassion you can show them this week.

Coaching Exercise: Love in Action

Choose one person to focus on today.

_____
_____
_____
_____
_____

What will you do to show them love in a Christlike way?

_____
_____
_____
_____
_____

Day

30

"Watch those runaway thoughts!"
Dr. B

Thoughts

"Finally, brethren, whatever things are true, whatever things are noble, whatever things are just, whatever things are pure, whatever things are lovely, whatever things are of good report, if there is any virtue and if there is anything praiseworthy—meditate on these things."

Philippians 4:8 NKJV

I'll never forget a Pastor asking us to memorize Philippians 4:8. Many of us grumbled—it was so long! But looking back, I'm grateful for his guidance. He emphasized why it mattered: aligning our thoughts and words with God's truth transforms us.

This verse calls us to focus on what's true, noble, and praiseworthy. Our thoughts can run wild, but God's Word acts like a guardrail, steering us back to what's good. Meditating on what pleases God is a daily choice, and it's worth it. Watch those runaway thoughts, and let God's truth guide you to a positive and fruitful mind.

Confession
I proclaim that I will do my best to keep my thoughts positive!

Prayer
Lord, please help me with my thoughts. Help me to think only the good things that I know will produce the results in my life that are pleasing to You.
In Jesus' name. Amen.

Reflection Moments: Thought Alignment Wheel

Label each section with one principle from Philippians 4:8 (true, noble, right, pure, lovely, admirable, excellent, praiseworthy).

Fill in the Sections:

Write down recurring thoughts in the corresponding sections where they align.

For thoughts that don't align, place them outside the circle.

Coaching Exercise: Thought Renewal Challenge

Choose One Misaligned Thought:
Identify a thought from outside the circle (example: I'm not good enough).

Rewrite the Thought: Replace it with a God-centered truth (example: I am fearfully and wonderfully made" Psalm 139:14).

_____
_____
_____
_____
_____

Create a motivational saying based on the new thought and recite it each morning.
Write this affirmation in multiple places (sticky notes, phone wallpaper) as a reminder.
Reflect on how focusing on this truth changes your mindset and actions throughout the week.

_____
_____
_____
_____
_____

Day

31

"God's Word prospers in the atmosphere."
Steve

Accomplished by God

"So shall My word be that goes forth from My mouth; It shall not return to Me void; But it shall accomplish what I please, And it shall prosper in the thing for which I sent it."
Isaiah 55:11 NKJV

His Word accomplishes exactly what He intends. God's words never return empty. His Word will prosper in your family when you fill your home with God's Word through prayer, reading scripture, and speaking His promises. It creates an atmosphere where faith grows, love deepens, and God's blessings flow. Trust that His Word will work in your family, bringing peace, unity, and strength. Speak His Word over every situation knowing that it will bring about God's desired change.

Confession
I declare that God's Word never fails. Everything He speaks over my life will be accomplished in His perfect timing and purpose.

Prayer
Lord, I thank You that Your Word is powerful and never returns empty. Help me to trust in Your promises, knowing that You will fulfill every word You've spoken. May Your will be done in my life, just as You have purposed.
In Jesus' name. Amen.

Reflection Moments: God's Word Milestone Map

Draw a Simple Path or Timeline.

Mark milestones along the way (Answered prayers, New revelations, Promises fulfilled).

For **each milestone**, briefly **note** what happened and the corresponding scripture.

Add a Future Milestone.
Leave space at the end of the path for a milestone you're trusting God to accomplish.

Coaching Exercise: Scripture Action Plan

Select a scripture that aligns with a specific area where you're seeking God for answers. (example: family unity, career breakthrough).

Create 3 action steps inspired by this verse.

Example: If the verse is about peace, action steps might include starting each day with prayer, reducing conflicts, or encouraging others.

_____
_____
_____
_____

Daily Accountability Check: Each evening, reflect: Did I take steps today that align with this verse? How did God's Word shape my actions and mindset?

Celebrate the Wins: At the end of the week, document how living out the verse impacted your life and those around you.

_____
_____
_____
_____

Day

32

"Simply love each other!"
Dr. B

What about love?

"Love is patient and kind. Love is not jealous or boastful or proud or rude. It does not demand its own way. It is not irritable, and it keeps no record of being wronged."
1 Corinthians 13:4-5 NLT

Intentional love isn't complicated. 1 Corinthians 13, known as the love chapter, gives us a visual of how to put love into our actions. It's easy to get caught up in our needs or react out of frustration.

We're called to be a reflection of God's heart. It's about letting go of irritations and offering grace. "Simply love each other" isn't just a phrase—it's a way of life that aligns us with God's purpose. Let's choose love today, letting it guide our words, actions, and attitudes.

Confession
I choose love.

Prayer
Lord, help me to love others as You do, with patience, kindness, and humility.
Let my actions reflect Your perfect love.
In Jesus' name. Amen.

Reflection Moments: Love Attribute Tracker

Prepare the Checklist:
Create a list of attributes from 1 Corinthians 13:4-5:
1) **Patience**, 2) **Kindness**, 3) **Not Envious**, 4) **Not Boastful**, 5) **Not Proud**, 6) **Not Dishonoring**, 7) **Not Self-Seeking**, 8) **Not Easily Angered**, 9) **Keeps No Record of Wrongs**,

Rate Yourself:
Next to each attribute, provide a 1-5 scale (1 = Needs Work, 5 = Doing Well).
Ask readers to rate themselves honestly for each attribute.

Coaching Exercise: Love in Action Challenge

Choose an Attribute:
Pick one attribute from the checklist where improvement is needed.

Set a Love Action Goal:

_____
_____
_____
_____
_____
_____

Write a specific way to practice this attribute today (example: If patience, "I'll take a deep breath and listen fully before responding to others.").

_____
_____
_____
_____
_____

Day

33

"Safety is found in the shelter of God's arms."

Dr. B

Finding a safe place

¹"He who dwells in the secret place of the Most High
Shall abide under the shadow of the Almighty. ²I will say of the Lord, He is my refuge and my fortress; My God, in Him I will trust."   Psalm 91:1-2 NKJV

I know personally what it means to live in Psalm 91. On a business trip, I was abducted, but God miraculously rescued me. I'll never forget that day because it changed my life forever.

Psalm 91:1-2 reminds us that true safety is found in the shelter of God's arms. When we dwell in His presence, He becomes our refuge and fortress. In every situation, we can trust Him to guard and guide us. Dedicating our families to God means placing them in His loving care, knowing He watches over us. Today, rest in the safety of His shadow and find peace in His protection.

Confession
I dedicate my family to God.
We will dwell in the secret place of the Most High, and we will trust in God as our refuge and fortress.

Prayer
Lord, I bring my family before You, knowing that we rest under Your protection. You are our refuge and fortress and we place our trust in You to guard and guide us through every situation. Keep us safe under the shadow of Your wings. We dedicate all that we are to You.
In Jesus' name. Amen.

Reflection Moments: Psalm 91 Scavenger Hunt & Blanket Fort

Scavenger Hunt:

Hide pre-written verses from Psalm 91 around your home.

Have each participant search for and collect the verses.

Blanket Fort Sharing:

Build a cozy blanket fort together.

Once inside, take turns reading the verses aloud, discussing what each verse means and how it brings comfort and protection.

Coaching Exercise: Safe Place Reflection

After sharing the verses, write or discuss how Psalm 91 reminds your family of God's protection.

_____
_____
_____
_____
_____
_____

End with a group prayer, dedicating your family to dwell in God's secret place of safety.

_____
_____
_____
_____
_____

Closing Thoughts

As you reach the end of this devotional, I hope you've felt God's presence in every step. We've explored three key tests of faith—Health, Wealth, and Family—areas that often challenge our trust and stretch our understanding. Each devotion was crafted to encourage you to rely more on God, to see His hand in the midst of your trials, and to embrace His promises even when circumstances don't change overnight.

Remember, faith isn't about having all the answers; it's about trusting the One who does. The interactive activities throughout this journey were meant to equip you with practical tools, but the true transformation happens in your heart. Our prayer has been this journey has shifted your perspective, allowing you to see God's faithfulness in every test and to respond with renewed hope.

Keep pressing into God's Word, holding onto His promises, and leaning on His strength. Your story is still unfolding and God is walking with you through every page.

May you continue to grow in trust, find peace in His provision, and experience the fullness of life He offers. Trust that He is at work. He is the Author and He is faithful.

About the Authors

B Austell, Ph.D., BCALC (Board Certified Advanced Christian Life Coach), is an accomplished multi-genre author, chaplain, coach, speaker, and founder of Simply B You®, a faith-based lifestyle brand encompassing beauty, books, coaching, and fitness. Dr. B holds a Ph.D. in Life Coaching and Counseling, a Master of Arts in Interdisciplinary Studies from Liberty University, where she focused on Public and Community Health, Life Coaching, and Exercise Science, and dual degrees in Interdisciplinary Studies from Georgia State University. Dr. B holds additional board-level certifications, including Senior Fellow Health and Well-Being: Fit for Christian Service and Fitness for Christian Seniors. Dr. B is also an ACSM/NPAS Physical Activity in Public Health Specialist, equipping her to integrate physical and spiritual wellness in her coaching practice.

With over 12 published works, including eight children's stories, Dr. B has passionately dedicated her career to helping individuals make Christ-centered, balanced lifestyle choices. Her expertise spans energy healing and management, brain health, financial freedom coaching, and trauma recovery. Since 1999, she has guided people to break barriers, overcome trauma-based decisions, and live with purpose and joy.

Steve Austell holds a Bachelor's degree in Religious Studies from the University of Tennessee and is the author of the wellness journal Vegetably Good. Formerly the President and CEO of Change for Jesus Ministries, Steve has dedicated his life to guiding others on their spiritual journeys. Now serving as a Chaplain and Entrepreneur, he encourages individuals to live balanced, faith-centered lives through a holistic approach to spiritual and physical well-being.

Connect with Us

Thank you for joining us on this journey of faith, growth, and breakthrough. We would love to stay connected with you!

Visit us online for more inspiration, resources, and updates:

YouTube: Simply Moments with Dr.B @SimplyBYou
Instagram: @SimplyBYouByDrB
Website: SimplyBYou.com
Steve's Etsy Shop: https://steveaustelldesigns.etsy.com

www.ingramcontent.com/pod-product-compliance
Lightning Source LLC
LaVergne TN
LVHW051606070426
835507LV00021B/2806